Earth

Wisdom

Meditations

111 Contemplations For People Who Love The Earth

by Judith Hirst

Earth Wisdom Meditations: 111 Contemplations For People Who Love The Earth

Library and Archive Canada Cataloguing in Publication

Hirst, Judith, 1954-
Earth Wisdom Meditations: 111 Contemplations For People Who Love The Earth

Nature--Religious aspects--Meditations.   I. Title.
BL624.2.H57 2011   204'.32   C2011-908000-1

ISBN: 987741306
EAN-13: 978-0-9877413-0-1

Published by Mission Earth Publishing
www.missionearthpublishing.com

Disclaimer

The publisher and author assumes no liability or responsibility for damage or injury to you, other persons, or property arising from any use of any product, information, idea, or instruction contained in the content or services provided to you through this book. Reliance upon information contained in this material is solely at the reader's own risk. The authors may have a financial interest in or receive compensation from manufacturers of products or websites mentioned in this book.

The editorial arrangement, analysis, and professional commentary are subject to this copyright notice. No portion of this book may be copied, retransmitted, reposted, duplicated, or otherwise used without the express written approval of the author, except by reviewers who may quote brief excerpts in connection with a review. United States laws and regulations are public domain and not subject to copyright. Any unauthorized copying, reproduction, translation, or distribution of any part of this material without permission by the author is prohibited and against the law. Disclaimer and Terms of Use: No information contained in this book should be considered as financial, tax, or legal advice. Your reliance upon information and content obtained by you at or through this publication is solely at your own risk.

Reviews

This is a meditation book like no other — for "Earth Wisdom Meditations" gently connects us to the vast and intricate web of energies that surround us. Judy's thoughts and words inspire us to open our mind and senses to these loving and supportive energies— which in turn enables us to 'hear', to 'notice', and to 'recognize' their soft murmurs.

Judy shares her understanding of this world with such empathy and compassion that one feels immersed with hope and encouragement. Her book is a gift of personal discovery; it provides us with insight into our own unique abilities, and we learn.

- Dianne Steen, Speech Instructor at Mount Royal University, Calgary, Alberta

"Earth Wisdom Meditations: 111 Contemplations for People Who Love the Earth" by Judith Hirst provides us with as opportunity to refocus on the connections we have with nature. As we meditate it reminds us to look, notice, wonder, accept ,and appreciate our world and our life. The individual passages enable us to look within, contemplate our lives, and let go of negative feelings.

Meditation #7, (my favorite) encouraged me to be open to new experiences, give up the need for control, be at peace, and learn serenity. One must accept life as it comes, and "Hang on for the Ride". As we progress through the life lessons we can become more in touch with our emotions, learn to accept and love ourselves. Focusing on one meditation can promote a new perspective on looking at the world within us and around us. This book provides us with an excellent guide to do just that.

- Aleda Sloane B.Ed., retired educator and nature lover

"Earth Wisdom Meditations" offers 111 short reflections based on images in nature. Author Judith Hirst links insights from the natural world to delve into our relationship with All That Is. These short meditations utter universal truths at many levels. All of life is interconnected in this collection. We are not alone, for we are created and creating. Take this book with you as you journey. Like the seed of meditation in #81, "Earth Wisdom Meditations" has the potential to manifest much growth. Less is more.

- Sharon Montgomery, author of Your Invisible Bodies: a reference for children and adults about human energy fields.
www.yourinvisiblebodies.com

In her book, "Earth Wisdom Meditations", Judy shows that the ways of the earth, nature, planets and stars can offer us insight and guidance if we are but open and receptive.

Sweetly written and inspirational, this book is a lovely source for reflection and for returning to the stillness and beauty of our own inner "earth" where all the answers lie"

- Luann Frances, Reiki Master, Shamanic & Holistic Healing Practitioner, Business owner, Eckville, Alberta

"Earth Wisdom Meditations" takes basic earthly things and explains it in a way that can be applied to daily living.

Each meditation is worth reading and contemplating. A great way to experience simple things in a better light!

- Phyllis Taylor "In Touch With You" Advanced Massage Therapist - Reflexologist Red Deer, Alberta

This is a truly beautiful book: truth is beautiful. I can say that everyone should read Earth Wisdom Meditations. Buy it for your children, give it to your friends, and certainly read it yourself, over and over.

- Jackie Branagan, Healer, Shaman, and Animal Communicator
www.dragonflyessence.com
dragonflyessence.blogspot.com

Acknowledgements

Thank you to everyone who reads my blog, angelsandancestors.blogspot.com, and have emailed me to say, "You need to write a book!" Your comments and your reactions to what I blogged was the prompt that got this project started.

Roger, my husband, thank you, for being there when I was tired and for making meals and for being supportive.

Thanks to my sisters, Pat and Barb, for their encouragement as I chugged along once I said that I would do this.

If friends are the vitamin, F, then I have some of the best Vitamin F in the world. My friends Sharon, Liane, Dianne, Rachel, Skye, Jackie, Aleda, Phyllis, Sharon (another Sharon), Diana, Lynne, Caroline, Bobbi, Maureen, Luann, Aleda, and Lisa have all cheered, pushed, suggested ideas, and supported me on this journey. I am grateful for your friendship.

To all those that have attended the New Moon Meditations that Roger and I host, thank you for telling me how the meditations that I do have eased your way so that you can do the work that you need to do.

To Sharon H. and to Gary V. - thanks for the help on putting this project all together. Your coaching made this less daunting.

Introduction

Some of the meditations I've included in this book come from my blog at angelsandancestors.blogspot.com

Other meditations were gifts from Creator or from Angels or from Guides. The meditations were given to me when I was thinking about something in Nature, and why the situation was the way that I saw it. The answer, in some cases, was "you are not seeing everything", and the scenes in Nature helped me to see the bigger picture. I hope that you are able to see the bigger picture through these words.

The meditations in this book are multipurpose. You can use them to focus as you go into meditation. If you have a question about something, open the book to see what meditation comes up for you. The meditations might even help you to see the relationship between the Earth and the person (others or yourself) and shed some light on the situation. Another way to use the meditation is to simply become the meditation. The words may be chanted, hummed, or repeated as part of a walking meditation. I often hear that meditation must be done this way or that way, or according to some special sitting requirement. Honestly, I believe that all forms of meditation are the right way. When we start putting limits on what we do, then, just possibly, we will miss something. Meditation can be done in silence, without any words. It can be done alone or as a group. Both types of meditation have power. Try all the ways.

Sometimes, we need words to express something that we see and want to share with others. The words in these meditations are meant as a synthesis of the patterns of Nature to what we as humans think and do. Perhaps the juxtaposition of one idea to another will feel like I am reaching.

The Earth is in a time of chaos. The sticky stuff that holds it together is love. Right now, so many people love the Earth and wish to care for it. I am amazed at the writings and actions of all these folks. A traditional name for people who love and honor the earth is "earth-keeper". These people, who send Mother Earth love on a daily basis, fight to keep her free from pollution, work tirelessly to protect her animals, and hassle governments and corporations to clean her waters. These meditations, I hope, will help you stay in the flow of all that is.

Sometimes we have to stretch to reach what we need. Simply allow the words to flow without judgment.

All meditations are given to you, the reader, as a blessing.

Love and light to all of you,

Judy

This is the time to practice wisdom.

1

One of the greatest gifts of wisdom is patience. The large Earth changes are upon us, and, they happen slowly. We animals see that the Sun and the Moon have moved in the sky. We see that there is more water in some places and much dryness in others. We are not ones to die off; we are survivors.

Let the mountain speak to you.

2

It called with force and dazzled with its light. It showed how one could climb up the path to converse with it. "Come!" it said. "I have things to say to you." The mountain said, "You hear me! Please come and converse with me so that I may speak. Only the stars are here with me, and we speak almost every night about mystery. I have so much to share, and stories to tell."

"The seasons are changing!" says the Robin.

3

"Pay attention, child! We are here one moon earlier than normal. Our food supply is changing. The weather shifts with the Earth. Do you not hear the grinding deep down in the ground, down below the worms? A big change is coming. We say that you are safe from the rocking ground. Make a strong nest!"

What is the love position?

4

It is easy! Love yourself. Love others. Love explains how your actions manifest in the surrounding world. Are you harmonious? Look at your relationships with others. Some are blessed. Some are not. Love them all!

I am the New Moon of Spring.

5

I am the gentle force that moves your oceans and seas. I call and pull out the power in your body, and ask it to shift to the energies that I send. Be still and feel the emotions swell in you as though they rose on the tide. Do not fear these changes. I am the light that carries you through the night. I send you dreams. I send you peace. I send you forgetfulness.

Motion carries you as you work through your purpose.

6

Purpose is simply taking action, doing what you know you need to do without the prompting or without following other's expectations. When you are in motion, you are searching. Although you may believe that you know the destination, along the way, it may change. So, watch for the signs that appear to you that signal changes in direction.

Let your emotions go; accept what is and that all you can do is 'hang' on for the ride.

7

Surrender and experience this period of time by not struggling! Be accepting! Be open and trusting to whatever new is coming your way for it is a gift. Do give up your need to control. Be at peace with that, and learn serenity. Accept the will of Creator. The Universe is One!

Do you need help?

8

Have you ever wished for an extra hand to push open a door when your arms are full of packages or parcels? Or, have you ever wished for a parking space close to the door of the mall, especially when it is raining? Close your eyes, and ask for help from all the Angels. Then, let them in. And, remember to give thanks.

You need a quiet mind so that ideas will have a chance of connecting.

9

Nature is full of ideas, and tries to share them with us. We do not hear them because our mind is busy. We do not see the shape (of the bush) that would be perfect for a new design. We miss the smell that is perfect for a new perfume. We rush through the world. To avoid frustration, simply be quiet.

I, The Universe, ask you to combat violence and disharmony.

10

Violence causes retaliation. So, I ask you to be kinder to yourself, and to those around you. As you do this, you will feel tension ease out of your body, and your stress will drain away. You will feel happy.

The Sun said "The Earth looks small!"

11

We are insignificant and great at the same time! If we did not exist, we would not celebrate the animals and their lives. We would not know about life flowing and ebbing, and rising slowly from the ground, up to the sky, to touch the Sun.

Isolated places!

12

This is the name that we give to places that Man cannot easily travel to. Yet, the birds and the animals and the creepy crawlies are there. They do not have the same restrictions that we place on ourselves. Open up yourself. Go to all places in your body and mind. Mimic the Earth.

Revenge has been around a long time.

13

This Latin proverb shows that it has been around as long as writing. "Revenge is a confession of pain". To truly understand the insidious power of revenge, look to something that Mahatma Gandhi said, "An eye for an eye would make the whole world blind." Inspire the world to see!

Anything that you can't see comes from the Devil! Is this true?

14

No. We do not see God, Love, Wind, Kindness, Oxygen, Carbon Dioxide, the sound of a Symphony, or anything one hears over the radio. Live in wonder of all the things that you cannot see.

Patterns of activity have meaning.

15

Patterns govern the movement of planets and plants. Patterns are balancing karmic events in the same way that big winds and rains clean the ground to leave no trace of passers-by. Every day we witness magic and mystery that flies over our heads because we do not understand. Accept!

The dandelion is like the Sun.

16

It brings healing. Our Ancestors used dandelion leaves or greens in the spring, to get the nutrients that were not available through the winter. Dandelion is a tonic - rich in vitamins, magnesium, iron and calcium. Breathe in the vitality of Dandelion. Let it nourish you.

Life is not fixed.

17

Be alert to whatever new opportunities cross your path. It may only happen once in your lifetime. Take time to stop and enjoy new things in your life. When you experience the world with the joy of a child, you will once again be awakened to the magic of creation.

The Pali word for meditation means "to make grow".

18

When I sit in meditation, I feel my ego become quiet, and I feel my soul grow upwards and outwards. I feel the roots of trees and grass take hold in the Earth. I feel the life around me. I am grateful.

Do not be afraid of adventure.

19

Being a risk taker keeps us interested in life and helps us stay alert for those who would prey on us (those who would use us to their own advantage). Trust! The flow of the adventure will bring you new insights into life, and insights into the mysteries of the forests, mountains, lakes and rivers. Allow!

Our Ancestors have always looked to the stars for guidance.

20

At some intuitive, or gut, level, they understood that the light required for human development and evolution, came from the stars. Archaeologists have discovered evidence that even 6000 years ago, humans were naming the stars. Look at the stars. What do the stars mean to you?

Mother Nature cleans up the plants and the trees for winter.

21

How would we clean up? Can you let go of old hurts, angers, resentments, and victimizations that hug your soul? These wounds, for they are wounds, cripple us because we cannot move forward in ease. The wounds may also cause us to become ill. Sit now, and allow old wounds to heal.

Consider Jupiter.

22

If we can see it, perhaps life on Jupiter sees us. Perhaps the light that Jupiter sends out to us is as vital to our growth and development as the light from the Sun. Unlike the Sun, we can gaze at Jupiter without damaging our eyes. Stare at it or imagine it now. Feel the light! Accept it into your body. Give thanks.

Moth flies by orienting to the Moon.

23

This is what scientists have determined. Moths fly by distance from a bright object. What bright object guides you? How do you stay oriented when all seems to be falling down around you? What keeps you going?

See yourself standing on a small ledge on a cliff.

24

You can go down without any help. However, to get up the cliff, you need help. This is a metaphor for life. Going down is easy. Going up takes faith and help from someone higher up

Drop a leaf on a river.

25

Watch it float, on the surface, down the stream. It will never try to swim upstream. It goes with the flow, sometimes following the current from side to side, and always moving forward. What stops you from moving forward, with the flow? Do you really want to go back to where you have been?

Find a quiet place and lie on the top of the grass or the snow.

26

How long has it been since you lay on the Earth? Since you were a child? Feel the ground pull the anxiety from you, and remember that you came from the Earth. It is part of you. The minerals in it are in you. Relax more deeply. Hear the sounds of the Earth, and feel comfort flow into your body.

Great Horned Owl sits on the north side of the tree during daylight when her eyesight is diminished.

27

She flies at night, when her sight is excellent. She has a rhythm to her movements. Where do you feel the rhythm in your life? Is it truly you, or someone else's dance that you are dancing?

Branches dry up as they mature, and will fall from the tree in a strong wind.

28

Our friends and family are often like dry branches. They drop from our lives as our relationship matures. We no longer need them, and they do not need us. It is the way it needs to be. Sometimes, just sometimes, there will be a seed on the branch that will grow when it drops in the earth. And, it starts its own tree.

A chair sized rock sits along a pathway.

29

Children climb on it. Creepy crawlies live under it, and call it home. Rain washes over it, keeping it clean. The rock is like many of us; it lives a simple life. The observer says that it endures. The real story is that it has adapted, and is content. Contentment is the offspring of love and peacefulness.

Berries grow in woodlands and fields.

30

Some are so very sweet while others are bitter. Some are just juicy, without much taste. People often seem like berries. They live in so many different places. Some people are tasty friends, and others are too sour for jam. Yet, in nature, all berries provide nourishment for some creature. All of us are needed.

Where do you find calmness when you feel that life is full of turmoil?

31

Close your eyes and think of a quiet breeze rustling the leaves of the poplar trees. Feel the gentleness of the murmur of the branches, pulling you from your thoughts. When you merge with the trees, then you can see what you need to do to resolve what causes the turmoil. You have a treetop view.

A sparrow's nest rests in the fork of the lilac bush.

32

It holds three eggs. Each egg has a potential. Each day is like an egg – filled with potential to be birthed and grow into something much bigger. Eggs need to be cared for otherwise they perish. How do you care for each day that is given to you?

The snow covers the land, unbroken except for grass and shrubs sticking up.

33

You are alone. Then you see footprints that could be a rabbit, or a mink, or a... You don't know what is out there. Even when we think we are alone, we are surrounded by so many things that we cannot see. They do not harm us. There is no reason to fear. Welcome the unseen.

Tiger lilies grow along the roadways and into the fields.

34

The bright orange triggers a memory of childhood. Orange was the best crayon. Orange juice was a treat. Carrots were fun to eat because they crunched. Orange is the color of imagination. Let your mind run with orange and feel the creativity flow.

Sit in meditation.

35

Call in the Archangels to hold the space and keep it sacred for you. Ask all your angels and guides, for the highest good, to come in and help you pull out all the jealousy and blame in your heart. Feel the freedom that comes from letting this go. Even if you want to hang on to it, let it go. It is time. Let it be done!

A path meanders through the field and into a stand of trees.

36

You can stand at the beginning of the path and imagine what it looks like when it gets into the trees. Until you walk it though, you will not see the flowers that grow along it, or the small animals that also use it. In fact, your imagination will not capture much of what is there. Stay in the present moment and enjoy the walk.

What is serenity?

37

It is the stillness of the lake in the early morning. It is the clear, smooth ice over the pond. It is the quiet on the deck in the evening. It is weeding the garden, or sitting and reading in the lawn swing. Serenity is where ever you connect with the Earth.

A waterfall thunders into the ground below, clearing the air.

38

The water laughs as it rushes down the giant slide. Getting close to the waterfall lets the water spray you with its freshness, and cleans your energies. Visit a waterfall, in person or in meditation. Ask it to clear you and wash away what troubles you at the moment.

The snow helps you to stay grounded.

39

It cleans the air. It cools off the energy of heat that is prevalent on the planet right now. It resets your body temperature and your body clock. Snow is good for you.

The Stone People line the bottoms of creek and river beds.

40

Their task is to guide the water down stream and to keep it from getting side tracked into the ground. Many stones get worn down from their task and sometimes, they end up breaking up into smaller pieces. Then they become something new. You are like the Stone People. Allow life to shape you.

The saying is, "As the crow flies."

41

This means that the distance is not quite straight, and that the destination takes you off the traveled roads. This is your quest – to travel along unknown paths and to create new paths. You will discover the core strength in yourself as you walk in new places. The trees will watch over you. You will be safe.

Find a place where you can go and rest and meditate.

42

It should not be your current house – someplace on the land. If you are scared of natural places, now is a good time to overcome that fear. Go there every day, and discover how sacred the place becomes.

I know that I am changing.

43

I change just as the Earth changes. I can feel it in my body and my head. I feel the expansion in my heart. The expansion tells me to look at the other parts of the story when I am upset at something that I judge to be an injustice or a hurt or a problem. And, my body relaxes.

I dream and I am on the edge of a swamp.

44

There were many white storks wading around in the water. From time to time, two storks would jump/fly together, and look like they were dancing. They way that they move their necks and wings is so creative that it seemed that they were ethereal beings, dancing away because life is so grand! I dream and I am grand.

When I sit in meditation, I always sit in protected space.

45

I reach out from my protected space and feel the land around me. I learn to listen to it, to determine what it needs, and how I can help it. If it needs me to weep for it, I do that. I am a caretaker for the Earth.

We have forgotten how to wait.

46

We can take lessons from the grass, and the trees, and the flowers. They have learned the lesson of patience over thousands of years. They understand the rhythm of life. We need to learn how to let things be. Today, I honor waiting.

The cold keeps you still.

47

There is a need for you to stay in place and in position. This allows you to be quiet and to be with yourself. It gives you time to contemplate what is currently going on in your life, and what needs to change. For some of you, visions of past times will begin to dance in your head.

What is a spiral?

48

How do you picture a spiral in your mind? Nature says that the spiral is the life force of all things. Hold this thought in your heart. Follow the spiral to see your life force.

Eostre, goddess, comes to Earth in the spring.

49

She provides support for the seeding, mating and birthing time. Any ventures started during this time will be very successful. Your project, business, or trip, will connect you with people that will help you define who you are for the next five to ten years. You are in a time of abundance.

Bear rambles, looking for food.

50

He remembers that there was rumbling in the Earth while he slept in his cave. The rumbling is new, as though the mountain is restless. Bear swings his head around. The birds are moving, heading north. Bear grunts as he wonders if all the land is in movement. Sit in stillness, and feel the movement.

I hear you. I hear your questions about the way things are.

51

I say to you that it need not be like this – no one needs to be hungry or without shelter. How people end up this way is by making choices. These choices are not right or wrong. I ask you to see further than seeing something as black or white. I ask you to see with compassion.

See further.

52

I see further than I did one million years ago. I see the beauty of the interaction of the organisms under my care. I too have learned to expand my compassion. And, I have learned that I must follow the natural processes. I will move forward with the changing of the land.

Healing cannot occur where there is no love or nurturing.

53

Healing cannot occur if the person is not in touch with Nature. If the human does not feel peacefulness and healing from the land, then there can be no Oneness. Great Spirit has provided all things so that we may all work, and may all be, in balance.

Dearest Beloved Beings! I wish to give you blessings.

54

I give you the blessing of being able to move on the path that is yours alone, without requiring the influence of others. I give you the blessing of rightness. I give you the blessing of self-love and self-approval. With these tools, you may accomplish anything. You are Creator!

Don't be content easily.

55

Allow yourself to walk further some days than others. Try new things. Spend time watching the bees on the flowers or the birds flying in the skies. You will observe a lesson, and you will have an "aha" moment. Feel your heart and mind grow.

The lightning rips open the clouds and rain falls.

56

This is like the anger that we feel, and the tears of rage that spill out of our bodies. This is really a profound release of grief. Like the lightning shoots from the clouds, shoot your grief into the ground. And then, rest!

Stand in the wind.

57

Close your eyes, and raise your arms to shoulder level. Turn so that your back is pushed by the elemental forces. Feel how they are a part of you. We are all connected by that which we cannot see – as we do not see the wind.

What is the act of swaying?

58

People sway. Elephants sway. Snakes sway. Branches sway. To sway is to dance to the pulse of belonging. Being contained means that you are not free to do what you will. Swaying, then, is a reaction to confinement. Are you swaying or do you walk freely?

Space around us is empty. Or, is it?

59

Do we see what is in the space around us – the light, the air, and the tiny organisms? We see only what our attention is drawn to. Today, pay attention to the invisible. The invisible fills up much of the world.

Softness can be protective.

60

The fuzzy leaves protect the young crocus as it pushes its way to the surface. The soft leaves protect the core plant from the harshness of frosts and of snow. Softness in all of us can protect us from taking all the world seems to throw at us, personally. We can let it all roll gently away from us.

Great Spirit places colors together in a random order.

61

There are not any restrictions about how colors are placed together, or how high up the mountain or down the valley that the colors can go. It just happens! Move outside the lines. We need to imagine with abandon. We need to color our world boldly!

As above, so below.

62

The Earth, too, is held in its place in this Universe by the gravitational pull of the Sun and the Moon and the push/pull of all of the other planets. It is a pattern so intricate that for thousands of years, no one believed it! The Catholic Church outlawed belief in it. Believe in the patterns of life!

The Sun is about illumination.

63

Is this the time to take courses or start a project on something that you have always wanted to do? Go for it! A great quotation is "You might say the Sun is symbolic of our ability to direct our will and to have a sense of purpose" – Melissa Osborne. Let the Sun guide your way.

Life is not an accident.

64

It is filled with glorious moments of synchronicities that have us meet certain people; get jobs that are the "dream job" that we have always wanted; and, have us feel tragedies that we feel drag us down that transform in to opportunities of great joy. I am a golden thread in the tapestry called life.

The color is white.

65

White is thought to represent light, goodness, purity and perfection. The color white also suggests faith and purity of spirit. Many believe that a white animal is a messenger from the Divine. Watch for white birds and animals. They honor the work that you do.

Chives signal spring's arrival.

66

The green is for healing, and for the heart chakra. The purple flower is for the crown chakra. It blooms early, and dies late in the fall. It flavors all that it touches, and it protects other plants from insects. Like a kind person, Chive is an honored herb.

A pond reflects back images.

67

It reflects the banks and foliage around it like the people around us reflect back our behavior. It is not about right and wrong. It is about seeing where our own behavior holds us back. Who is mirroring you right now?

I see a waterfall.

68

It falls easily and steadily. This motion takes me to a place of stillness that allows me to be so in the present moment that I forget where I am. Being this present, for me, is living in sanctuary. Being in this place is peaceful, joyous, and restoring.

The mountain looks inaccessible.

69

Yet, the mountain goats and sheep depend on it for both food and for protection. We do not need to blast down the mountain so it is easier to climb. We need only to find the best trail, up or down. And, we can become one with the mountain.

Smell the tang of the juniper bush.

70

Juniper bushes are planted at thresholds to keep the home from harm. For this reason, juniper is one of the sacred plants. It is used for smudging. When you feel frightened call on juniper for protection.

A Loon calls out at dusk.

71

If offers a benediction for the coming night. It sings of water lapping at the shore. It tells tales of fishing. It shares the contentment of life that is simple. Now, turn your focus inward. Find that contentment within yourself.

What is aloneness?

72

Every place we go, there is something. Aloneness does not exist, except in our minds. We look at Nature, and we see that no animal walks alone for it is surrounded by birds, by animals, and by what is in the Earth. We are interconnected. We cannot be alone.

After the storm, the air feels fresh.

73

When we move out from under our guilt and resentment, we lift the storm from our lives. The clouds clear. We open up for the light of the Sun and healing happens. We become stronger, like a new shoot that becomes a flower bearing plant.

Who is the master of the trees?

74

No one. Trees are unique, and of themselves. Trees stand tall, bending before a storm, falling only if they are unhealthy. There is no need to tell them what to do. They are perfect, and do what is coded in them. We, too, are perfect. We need no master.

Stillness.

75

It helps the Mouse hide from the Hawk. It camouflages the Rabbit into the landscape. It is counter to movement. Stillness appears throughout the natural world. Often, humans see stillness as confinement. It is a glorious part of life. Be at peace with stillness.

The forest is gone!

76

Three hundred years or more, of large trees – gone. The fire had left few blackened trunks and much ash. In the desolation, young jack pines are brilliant against the black. Fire is needed to release their seeds. Death and rebirth – the cycle continues.

A cave is a portal.

77

It takes us to the underworld where stalagmites and crystals are formed; and it leads us to the underground water pathways. The cave represents the dark, unknown part of us. Today is a good day to walk into the cave and see the treasures that it holds.

Everybody is afraid of being nothing.

78

Look around at Nature. Everything has meaning. There is no thing that does not have a purpose. Each animal, rock, tree, or plant, has its own unique pattern that supports some other part of nature. So, too, it is with us. We are all needed.

Why do you ask others to change you?

79

See the small animals and birds and insects. They are as they are. They follow their nature. No one tells them that they are wrong. They do not need to change. Look inside. You, too, have your pattern in Nature. Walk that path.

Waves crash on the shore.

80

Each wave hits the rocks or the beach with its own intensity, and yet, each is part of the whole. We are all like that. We struggle with our journey, and we are caught up in the hype. Though we ignore one another, we are, however, part of the wave of humanity. Feel the comfort of the waves.

Seeds are great teachers.

81

While it may look inconsequential, even the smallest seed may grow to something many times its size because it follows its nature. Each seed grows, looking for the light. It gathers all the nourishment that it needs – no more, no less. Hold a seed and observe its perfection.

Clouds gather overhead.

82

I look up and see faces in the shapes of the clouds. I see some friends and then some loved ones. And then the Angel appears in the clouds. I know that they are well and taken care of. I am comforted.

Trout jumps in the river.

83

She says, "Highs and lows are normal in life. Everyone is looking for balance – the balance is to allow both, and not stay in one place or the other. Two highs balance two lows; warmth balances coolness. We all need both."

What is a weed?

84

Once, it was the name for herbs or grass. Now, it means "unwanted". Contemplate all those things in your life that you consider to be weeds. Now, thank them. They have helped you grow.

See the weeping willow.

85

It weeps not for sadness. It weeps for joy! It has food, water, and companions. Life, for the willow, is perfect. Find the perfection in your life, and honor it. Be like the willow and see joy.

A rainbow crosses the sky.

86

To see a rainbow is to be reminded that any distance may be bridged. A conflict is a distance between two people. Call on the magic of the rainbow to bridge the distance. Allow the healing.

Spirit rock.

87

All over the world, people have sacred sites called Spirit Rock – Ayers Rock, Stone Mountain, Stonehenge – to name a few. Meditate on a spirit rock. Feel the wisdom and the truth that is stored there.

Walk in a ploughed field.

88

Note that it is easy to trip. You must watch where you step. Ploughing prepares the ground for new crops. Do you need to plough up a part of your life to prepare it for something new?

Hail!

Little balls of ice. It represents ideas frozen in time, frozen emotions, and stillness. Hail carries frozen light to the ground. Each ice ball sparkles with energy. Be like the hail and melt to release what is frozen in you.

Stones pave the way.

90

By itself, one stone may be a barrier or hindrance to walking forward. However, many stones together will create riverbeds, pathways, and sign posts for us to follow. Watch for signs from the stones around you.

Feathers are gifts.

91

Feathers promise that Creator has heard your prayer, and that the Angels will deliver. Birds love to be part of this service, and cheerfully drop their feathers on your doorstep or path to assist the Angels.

Hear the ocean in a shell.

92

Why do we hear the ocean in this small object? Everything is found in smaller objects. Like the ear represents the human body, the shell represents the entire ocean. Think about this miracle.

A stick lies on the ground.

93

When you pick it up and walk with it, it becomes a staff. It supports you and protects you. The stick transforms when it works in service. We, too, transform when we work in service to others.

Dew bathes the grass.

94

It is dawn, and the sun rises. Sunlight sparkles in the moisture on the grass making the meadow look like heaven sparkling with light. Beads of water create prisms that create rainbows. It is a rainbow meadow.

Dust twists up to the sky.

95

Wind and sand play together and tumble over the land. In the process, sand migrates from place to place, as the wind wills. Together, they cause change. If you could shift with the wind, where would you go?

The glacier groans.

96

We see it shift slightly. A huge, grinding, thundering noise drowns out all other sound. A chunk breaks off the wall of ice. A new ice berg is birthed! It rocks back in forth in the waves. Our ship backs up. Any birth is beautiful!

Boom, boom.

97

The beat is the rhythm of the Universe. There is someone who will always hear it. The Beat is the heartbeat of Creator/Creation. The sound is a steady one-two-three-four-five-six-seven-eight beat, played over and over. It strengthens us and balances us. Listen to the beat.

Let go!

98

Hanging on is not going to help the process of change. Let go! Feel the oceans of oneness and joy that will move through your home, career, and leisure. Feel a moment of Zen, where nothing matters. Your Soul will guide you!

I hear chanting at night.

99

It is coming from a faraway place. It sounds like monks chanting very old sounds. I find comfort in the rhythm of the sound. The chant is for peace for each individual, for humanity, and for the planet. The sound of the night lulls me to sleep.

The Earth moves.

100

Black dirt boils up from the ground as the mole clears her tunnel. Nature's servant aerates and replenishes the top soil. Mole does this without thought. It is right. We need to be like Mole and do what is right, without internal debate.

What is desire?

101

A salmon returning to its stream of spawning, to mate and to propagate, shows desire. It moves with single purpose, not eating, and fighting other salmon, along the way. It struggles, rests, and moves on. It shows us purpose.

Create a garden.

102

Feel the life force of the Earth. Watch the seeds that you scatter grow into beautiful plants. It is easy to feel connectedness to plants when you have done the work. Friendships are like that. To feel connected, you must work on the friendship.

Smell the fresh mown grass.

103

This smell transports us to summer. It means that the sun is shining, and all is growing. People seem happier in the summer, perhaps from the warmth of the sun or because they are not constrained by volumes of clothes. Summer then, means freedom.

We say our lives unravel.

104

It is true. If you watch plants grow, you see that the stalk unravels, or furls outward. Leaves unravel outward. Unraveling is about gaining more life. One is less contained. Welcome the unraveling into your life. It is time for you to grow.

Lava bubbles in the volcano.

105

When the pressure becomes too high, the mountain spews lava, destructively, in all directions. What is in its path is destroyed. This same lava, at a deeper level, heats pools gently to give us healing baths. Some say lava is like anger. Is yours destructive or healing?

We all crave sweetness.

106

Animals will seek out honey and ripe fruit. Sweetness nourishes and soothes. In that moment, eating something sweet, we are truly present. Humans or animals are completely caught up in the act of enjoyment. Transfer that feeling to other parts of your life.

A bouquet of flowers!

107

Brides carry them, they decorate our tables, and they fill our gardens. Do flowers come to our celebrations to honor us? Or, did we create celebrations so that we could bring in Nature, and honor it? What we show is that we are incomplete without Nature. Thank it now.

What is quicksand?

108

It is a blend of water and sand that yields to pressure, and therefore, animals will sink in it. It is like deceit. Too many lies turn a situation into a trap that leaves the lie-teller sinking. Loved ones abandon the person. Now is a good time to get rid of any quicksand in your life.

The Sun sets behind the clouds.

109

The sky fills with shades of pink and purple. It is the crowning moment of the day. Then, darkness! Sunset is like a moving line of energy that diminishes as it travels, until it is gone. It represents life, and death. It is who we are.

Love the Earth!

110

To begin to love is to start to heal, say the Shaman. To love is to be without judgment. Just as we judge others and try to change them, so have we judged the Earth, and tried to remake her. Let us undo that now. Let us move back from interference. Move to acceptance, of the Earth and of Self.

I wish you a moment of sanctuary.

111

I wish for you a moment of joy where you can walk with the magnificent Presence and feel a peace so profound that it opens your heart chakra. May you hear the music of the spheres and have harmony for every day of your life.

Learn More About Spirit Animals, Spirit, and Angels

You <-> The Earth <-> Its Inhabitants

Angels, Action Items, Alligator, Antelope, Buddha, Bear, Buffalo, Change, Camel, Cattle, Deer, Dependencies, Dog, Dolphin, Elephant, Emotions, Eagle, Elk, Feelings, Fox, Frog, Fear, Goose, Gorilla, Great Spirit, Hawk, Heron, Healing, How To.....Mediations, Prayers......

Check out all of the FREE information in over 1,000 blog posts at:

Angelsandancestors.blogspot.com (since 2007)

For more information about other books from this author, visit: www.missionearthpublishing.com/authors

About The Author

Judith Hirst currently lives in Calgary, Alberta, Canada, with her husband, Roger, and their two dogs, Magic and Sage.

She loves to be out in the parks or along the rivers, with the animals and the trees. Judith shares her insights on her blog, which she writes daily at:

Angelsandancestors.blogspot.com

She also teaches various classes including the StarTalker Quest program.

See www.angelsandancestors.com for more information on upcoming events.

Made in the USA
Charleston, SC
30 January 2012